Reading is Believing

Developing Critical Reading Skills and Strategies

By

David R. Smith, NBCT

Amazon Press

New York

For my students,

Past, Present, and Future

ISBN: 978-1721982127

Printed in the United State of America

TABLE OF CONTENTS

~~~

PART 1: Reading Skills and Comprehension

PART 2: Organizational Aids and Response Questions for Reading and Writing

WORD STRATEGIES

Welcome, readers! Glad you could join me on this journey into the wonderful world of words. Let's jump right in, shall we?

If you're going to read anything, you need to know how to say the words. I don't mean the little ones, I mean those *gnarly* words that tie our tongues into knots. Good readers use strategies to figure out how to say them and what they mean.

For example, if the word is *spoil* and you know the /oi/ sound, it will help you read the word. You can also think of word families: if you know the word *oil* just add the /sp/ and the word becomes *spoil*.

If you don't know how to say the word or you don't know what the word means, reread the sentence and use context clues to help you figure out the word or meaning. You may have to reread the sentences before and after to find clues.

- For instance, try to substitute a synonym (a word which means the same or nearly the same). Look at the following sentence:

    If you don't know what to do, I can **assist** you.

    If you don't know what the word "assist" means, say the sentence using another word that makes sense:

    If you don't know what to do, I can **help** you.

    The word *assist* means help.

Let's Play Word Detective!

Read each sentence below out loud. Figure out the meaning of each underlined word by choosing a synonym to replace it. List the clue words that helped you figure out what the word means.

1.) Andrea was a very ***impertinent*** young lady. She always talked while her teacher was explaining a lesson. She showed no respect for other students. Her manners were very poor. Even her parents thought that Andrea was impolite.

A synonym for **impertinent** might be _____

What were your clue words? _____   _____   _____

2) The jungle we were traveling through was ***treacherous***, full of hidden risks and deadly animals.

A synonym for **treacherous** might be_____

What were your clue words? _____   _____

3) We traveled over rough ***terrain***. The mountains were tall and hard to climb, and quick sand was all over the place.

A synonym for **terrain** might be _____

What were your clue words? _____   _____

INDEPENDENT WORK—Vocabulary Detective

In each box below, copy a passage from the book or article you're reading that has a word whose meaning you're unsure of.

A synonym for _____ might be_____

What were your clue words? _____

A synonym for _____ might be_____

What were your clue words? _____

MORE WORD STRATEGIES

We just talked about sounding out the words by using the word families we know.

- For example, if the word is spoil and you know the /oi/ sound, it will help you say the word more quickly.
- You can also think of word families- if you know the word *oil* just add the /sp/ and you know the word is *spoil*.

We also talked about context clues, how re-reading the sentence and the ones that come before and after can give you clues to help you figure out the word meaning.

Now, we're going to add one more, because when you read non-fiction, you're going to come across new and longer words you've never seen before. We need a way to decode long words with a lot of **syllables.**

Let's call our strategy the Connect the Dots strategy.

> *Syllable*
>
> *a unit of speech sound*

Think of the word "helicopter."

The word has four speech sounds: hel / i / cop / ter
                                       .   .   .   .

We know it has these four parts because it has 4 vowels that we can either hear or see—in this case, an r-controlled vowel pattern (er).

We put a dot under each of those vowels then figure out where to divide the word into syllables. We divide up the word so there is *only one dot* in each syllable. (Note: when there is a vowel team, like /ai/ in rain, you give the team only 1 dot because it makes one sound. I like to underline the team and put the dot under the line)

Try "connecting the dots" the same way with the words below. Then I'll show you a little trick to make this strategy even easier!

riveting   riptide

chocolate   blizzard

streaming   handsome

Remember:
If a vowel doesn't sound right in a word, flip it and try again!

You do NOT put a dot under the silent -e at the end of any of the words. That -e is there to make the vowel before it long. Most words above get two dots, but 2 words have three syllables. That means those words get 3 dots.

As you no doubt know, many words are much longer and harder to decode than these. This isn't a problem, however, because many of our longest words are built with what are called **prefixes** and **suffixes**.

Look at the next two pages to help you understand what these are and how to tell them apart.

Prefix

a word part added <u>in front of</u>
a base word to change the meaning

Prefix	Meaning	Examples
re-	again	rewrite
un-	not	unkind
pre-	before	premade
dis-	not, opposite of	dishonest
im-	not, opposite of	impolite
non-	not	nonsense
mis-	wrong, bad	misbehave

SUFFIXES

-COME AT THE END OF A WORD
-CHANGE THE MEANING

SUFFIX	MEANING	EXAMPLE
-s, -es	more than one; verb maker	Character**s**, reach**es**
-ed	in the past; quality, state	walk**ed**
-ing	doing something; quality, state	walk**ing**
-ly	how	safe**ly**
-er, -or	one who; action; compares	drumm**er** dishon**or** bigg**er**
-tion -sion	noun: quality, action	ten**sion** distrac**tion**
-able, -ible	able to be	revers**ible** cap**able**
-al, -ial	related to, like	part**ial**
-ance	quality, state, action	resist**ance** dist**ance**

Now that we know what prefixes and suffixes are, let's see how we can mark a word now and read it.

Let's take the word "respectable."

First things first. We'll mark the word with our dots under each vowel we hear or see as part of a team:

respectable
.   .   .   .

This word is a four-syllable word. Now we'll get in the habit of being close readers and looking for syllables like prefixes and suffixes. We find two in this word: re- and -able. We'll put a box around the prefix and suffix:

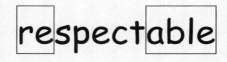

re spect able
.   .   .   .

Caution:

No strategy is perfect. If this strategy isn't helping you with a word, stop and look closely again. There may be something you're missing, like a little word you know tucked inside a bigger one.

Now we can decode the word properly:

re / spect / a / ble

You may be thinking, *I can already read all these words without doing this,* and I'm sure you're right. However, as you read non-fiction text, new words you've never seen before will show up. Now you have a way of attacking them so you can read them correctly.

Mark the words below the way you were shown to do. Read them out loud and then to somebody else when you are done.

overcome	conversation	dictionary
macaroni	refreshment	raspberry
strawberry	gingerbread	reflection
refrigerate	mountain	uncommon
resistance	indecisively	adversely
watermelon	helicopter	musical
alphabetize	revolutionize	immunity

P.S. Remember the vowels are a, e, i, o, u and sometimes y!

In each box below, copy a passage from the book or article you're reading that has tricky words to pronounce. Then write the words on the lines below and decode them with your new reading strategy.

Answering Questions

This may seem like a funny section to include in a book of reading strategies. After all, what's so hard about answering questions? The teacher asks the question and you give the answer, right?

Well, sort of, yeah.

Except you probably have noticed that teachers want some answers written a certain way. Sometimes teachers want "short responses" and other times "long responses."

What's the difference? How much do you write and how do you know when you're finished?

Those are good questions, and we're going to tackle them now.

Very Short Answers

Sometimes you only need to give a one- or two-word response. The best way to know that is by how much line space you've been given to use.

A question might look like this: *How old are you?* _____

You're not expected in this case to write more than a number or word. If you were expected to write more, the line would be longer.

Short Answers

Many questions fall under this category. These are questions that require a sentence or two to answer.

The important thing to remember with these questions is that most of the time **the teacher wants complete sentences.** This means you don't just give a few words to answer the question, but you put those words in a complete sentence, usually by borrowing some words from the question.

For example: What is your favorite food? _____

_____

You might answer like this: *My favorite food is cheese pizza.*

Notice what happened here. The first three words were dropped, and the key words *favorite food* were used. You can do this most of the time with questions. Just cross off the question words and find the key words in the sentence.

Try these two examples.

What is your favorite subject in school? _____

_____

How do you get to school every day? _____

_____

Short Answers ... with description

Sometimes you will be asked a question that wants you to describe an event, or something that happened to you or a character in a story, etc.

For example:

Describe your favorite restaurant. _____

_____

_____

Notice the number of lines this time. Most of the time, 3 lines = *minimum* two complete sentences. The other important point to note is the word *describe*. How do we describe anything? Simple, really. We write sentences that tell who, what, where, when, why, and possibly how something happened.

Let's try it with the question above.

My favorite restaurant is Pizza Hut in Canandaigua. (who, what, where) *My family takes me there for dinner on Friday nights,* (who, when) *and we sit in the back corner booth next to the window because we love the view.* (where, why)

See? Two sentences, but lots of details. Very descriptive. You could make it even more descriptive about the restaurant and what you like about it, but you were only give a few lines. Therefore, two sentences are usually enough—unless your teacher asks for more, of course. ☺

Short Answers ... with description, cont'd

Sometimes you have to write a descriptive response, but the directions don't explicitly tell you to describe.

For example, you might be asked to list important details or steps in a process, explain something, or give reasons why something happened.

For example:

Why did Goldilocks enter the Bear family's house? _____

_____

_____

_____

_____

Notice there are four whole lines to answer this question. Four lines = *minimum* 3 complete sentences. Since this is a "why" question, you need to tell the reason Goldilocks broke into the bear family's house and describe what made her do it in the first place. You might need evidence from the text. Or you may need to make an inference and use some of your own background knowledge and experience to answer it.

Let's give it a shot.

Goldilocks entered the bear family's house through the front door because she was curious. (who, what, how, why) *She was walking through the woods one morning by herself when she discovered the house.* (who, what, where, when) *Bored, she decided to check it out and see what was inside.* (why, who, what)

Text-based Answers

Text-based responses are not as tricky as they sound. You're simply answering a question using details straight out of a book, passage, article, etc. This means you can't just say what you think—you must include words in your answer as they're written in a text. This is called citing the text. You must use quotation marks when you cite a text.

There is a strategy that you can learn to help you understand how to answer this type of question. That strategy is called RACES, which stands for:

Read the whole question

Answer all parts

Cite the text

Explain your answer

Summarize

Read the following short passage and the question that follows.

    To Jacob's left he spotted the black-iron gate surrounding the village cemetery. The legends warned that the spirits there were restless and would chase away anyone who entered the graveyard at night. It was said an old witch named Miranda lived in the woods near the cemetery. People were afraid to walk alone at night in the woods. The legends spoke of her power to change shape and cast spells. She could even bring famine and disease to those she didn't like.

Why were people afraid of the woods at night? _____

_____

_____

_____

_____

_____

_____

Notice this question has six whole lines, so we're expected to write a *minimum* of 3-4 sentences. To begin to answer this question, we need to closely read the passage. It may take at least TWO readings to understand the main idea and the key details. Remember: we must "quote" from the passage to answer the question completely.

Here is a sample answer and how I used RACES to write it:

People were afraid of the woods at night because of the witch, Miranda. **(R, A)** *In the text it states, "She could even bring famine and disease to those she didn't like." **(C)** Farmers wouldn't have wanted to risk making the witch angry because she could have ruined their livelihoods. **(E)** Therefore, the farmers would have stayed away from the cemetery and woods at night. **(S)***

Notice that the **R** in Races is simply Read the Whole Question. The question only has one part to it: Why were people afraid of the woods at night? That means the A, C, E, S each needs at least one sentence, making this a four-sentence response.

Website Woes

Gina Murphy was exhausted when she got home from school. Her sixth-grade computer teacher had assigned the class a long project to do over the weekend—design a website! How was she going to finish it by Monday? She was so worried, her stomach started to cramp. When she got home, she plopped in a chair in the living room and closed her eyes.

"Everything all right?" she heard her mother ask.

Gina opened her eyes. Her head pounded with a headache.

"Not really," she admitted. Her mom sat down across from her, and Gina told her all about the assignment.

"Oh, that's okay," Mrs. Murphy said. "I can help you."

"This project is going to take me forever!" Gina groaned, turning away. "I barely know how to type on a computer!"

"Why don't you rest a while," suggested Mrs. Murphy, "and we'll talk about it more over dinner. I have a few ideas."

Gina's mouth watered when she smelled something spicy wafting from the kitchen. "What are we having?"

"Your favorite—spaghetti and meatballs!"

At dinner, Gina's parents helped her plan for her computer project.

"You know, your father and I both work for a tech firm, so we know a lot about websites and how they work."

Gina's eyes grew wide. "You do? I thought you just typed stuff all day."

Mr. Murphy laughed as he pushed his empty plate aside. "We do that, too. But I also write software programs that run many of our company's systems. Your mother works on our company's cyber security programs to be sure all of our data is secure. Big league stuff, kiddo."

Wow. Gina had never really asked what her parents did all day, except she knew they drove to work at a big shiny building in the middle of the city. And worked on computers.

"So, you guys can help me design a website?"

"You betcha," said Mrs. Murphy. "We'll get to it right away!"

After dishes were washed and put away, Mr. and Mrs. Murphy led Gina to her mother's office. They let her sit at her mother's enormous desk and turn on the computer.

"You design a website using a platform," explained Mrs. Murphy as she logged in. "An example of an easy platform to use is Wix."

"That's right," added Mr. Murphy. "You can build a website for free using Wix and add lots of cool features to it. Check it out."

Together, Gina's mother and father showed her all the background designs and layout options for her website. Gina chose colors and themes, and then she typed a short description about herself for the home page. Later, her mother promised to show her how to upload photographs and text.

"Thank you so much for your help, guys," Gina said with a smile.

"Anytime," said her mother. "There's just one more thing. Your website needs a domain name, an address to type into the search engine to find it. What do you want to call your website?"

Gina thought for a moment. "I think I have a great idea!" She started typing www.ginahastwogreatparents.com.

Laughing, her parents high-fived her and agreed it was a great name.

Comprehension Questions

1. Who is the protagonist in the story? _____

2. What assignment did the teacher give her? _____

    _____

3. Why is Gina so exhausted? _____

    _____

4. Use RACES to answer the following question.

    How did Gina's parents help her with her school project?

    _____

    _____

    _____

    _____

    _____

    _____

    _____

Fantasy or Realistic?

As you may have noticed, stories can be realistic or fantasy. They can take place in a character's backyard, or in a galaxy far, far away (just ask Luke Skywalker). Can you tell the difference?

<u>FANTASY</u> – a story that could not happen in real life. This genre includes fairy tales, folktales, fables, and science fiction. Animals may talk or have other powers. These are stories of pure imagination.

<u>REALISTIC FICTION</u> – A story that could happen in real life. Fiction in which the basic story elements seem real.

What are the basic story elements?

- Setting – Where and when the story takes place.

- Plot – What happens in the story.

- Dialogue – What is said in the story.

- Characters – Who the people and/or animals are in the story.

Let's read the following two stories and then answer a couple questions. Can you figure out which one is realistic fiction and which one is fantasy?

Excerpt from the novel <u>A Trunk of Trouble</u> by David R. Smith

The bus dropped me off as usual in front of Grandma's house. I waved good-bye to my friends and wandered up the sidewalk to Grandma's front door. Inside, the air was cool and sweet-smelling. Grandma kept lots of plants and flowers all over the place. She even taught me the names of most of them. To some people, Grandma's house might appear cluttered, but she just loved to collect beautiful things. Which, she once told me, made a house a home and life worth living.

I found Grandma nestled in her favorite reading chair in the living room. All the windows were thrown open. The rain had stopped a couple hours ago, and sunlight spilled onto the floor like puddles of liquid gold. A gentle breeze ruffled the curtains. Grandma looked up at me as I entered the room.

"*Bonjour*!" she called cheerfully. Grandma liked to use foreign words when she talked. She especially liked French, because it was the language of love and romance, she explained. I thought love and romance were pretty icky, but I didn't say anything. Adults were too weird sometimes to understand kids.

"*Comment vas-tu*?" I replied. That meant, "How are you?" Grandma taught me that one last week.

"I'm well, thank you." She smiled. "How was school today?"

I shrugged and plopped down on the sofa across from her. "Okay."

She frowned. "Just okay? Usually for you that means something happened at school. You didn't draw any pictures of monsters eating the class again, did you?" I giggled and shook my head. She remembered the time I made Billy Blake look like a huge hairy beast in order to embarrass him and make him leave Brookstone Elementary. That was last fall, when he first came to our school. My plan, of course, backfired in a big way, but at least I got a new friend out of the deal.

"There's a chance I might have bitten off more than I can chew," I told her. This was one of Grandma's favorite figures of speech. Like most figures of speech, it planted a clear image in my mind. Whenever I heard it, I visualized a little kid with a huge turkey drumstick stuck in his mouth.

"Tell me about it," she said. I told her about it. All of it. The talent show, Andrea Miller … and my big mouth.

Grandma nodded thoughtfully. "Seems like the Flanagan curse has struck you again."

"If by that you mean I let my temper get the best of me, I guess you're right."

"This time might be more serious than the last," she pointed out.

"What do you mean?"

Grandma leaned forward. "Now you've got your friends involved. If you don't find some way to make an elephant disappear, they're going to get laughed at just like you."

I never thought about it that way before. I guess I needed to be more careful about what I said and who I involved in my plots. I thought about Nolan, sitting there on the bus like the loneliest kid in the world. Then I remembered his quarter sitting in my pocket. Poor kid. Guess I'd better return that to him tomorrow.

The Fox and the Crow
By Aesop

One bright morning as the Fox was following his sharp nose through the wood in search of a bite to eat, he saw a Crow on the limb of a tree overhead. The lucky Crow held a bit of cheese in her beak.

"No need to search any farther," thought sly Master Fox. "Here is a dainty bite for my breakfast."

Up he trotted to the foot of the tree in which the Crow was sitting, and looking up admiringly, he cried, "Good-morning, beautiful creature!"

The Crow, her head cocked to one side, watched the Fox suspiciously. But she kept her beak tightly closed on the cheese and did not return his greeting.

"What a charming creature she is!" said the Fox. "How her feathers shine! What a beautiful form and what splendid wings! Such a wonderful Bird should have a very lovely voice, since everything else about her is so perfect. Could she sing just one song, I know I should hail her Queen of Birds."

Listening to these flattering words, the Crow forgot all her suspicion as well as her breakfast. She wanted very much to be called Queen of Birds, so she opened her beak wide to utter her loudest caw, and down fell the cheese straight into the Fox's open mouth.

"Thank you," said Master Fox sweetly, as he walked off. "Though it is cracked, you have a voice sure enough. But where are your wits?"

The flatterer lives at the expense of those who will listen to him.

Now that you've read both stories, try answering the following questions.

1. Which story is the realistic one? _____ Go back and highlight 3 examples of realism in the text.

2. Which one is fantasy? _____ Go back and highlight 3 examples of fantasy in the text.

3. How can you tell the difference? _____

_____

Show a friend or family member the examples you highlighted. Be sure to explain which details are fantasy and which ones are realistic and how you know the difference!

<table>
<tr><td>Vocabulary
Review</td></tr>
<tr><td>synonym</td></tr>
<tr><td>fiction</td></tr>
<tr><td>narrative</td></tr>
<tr><td>realistic</td></tr>
<tr><td>fantasy</td></tr>
<tr><td>text structure</td></tr>
<tr><td>plot</td></tr>
<tr><td>setting</td></tr>
<tr><td>cause/effect</td></tr>
<tr><td>sequence</td></tr>
<tr><td>visualize</td></tr>
<tr><td>inference</td></tr>
<tr><td>trait</td></tr>
<tr><td>figurative language</td></tr>
<tr><td>theme</td></tr>
<tr><td>main idea</td></tr>
<tr><td>summarize</td></tr>
</table>

Text Structure

Text structure refers to the way that authors organize their story. Learning to recognize the underlying structure of **texts,** like personal narratives and **fiction,** can help you focus on key ideas, predict what's to come, and check your comprehension as you read.

There are many, many narrative text structures. Below are seven you should be aware of and learn to recognize. You are likely to find one of these structures in every chapter or picture book you read.

1. **Problem and Solution**: This cause-and-effect text structure involves a character with a problem who is trying to solve it and achieve a goal. This is the *most common structure* in narratives. Before you get half way through the story, you should be able to identify what the problem is and how the characters are trying to solve it. (See example on page 30)

2. **Circular**: In a circular text, the action begins and ends in the same place. Think Jan Brett's *The Mitten* or Laura Numeroff's *If you Give a Mouse a Cookie.* By the time you reach half way in the story, you should be able to give examples of the cause-and-effect link in the plot and predict how the story will end.

3. **Cumulative**: Using lots of repetition, these stories add layers of new details to previous ones, and each text section repeats all the previous details. An example would be the children's book, *There was an Old Lady who Swallowed a Fly.* Before you get half way through the story, you should be able to explain how the details are adding up.

4. **Diary**: Stories told as diary or journal entries. For example, *Diary of a Wimpy Kid* and *Diary of a Worm*. You should be able to notice the dated heading at the beginning of each section and notice patterns in the timeline.

5. **Framing-Question Text**: This is text focused around one central question in the beginning. Think *Snowmen at Night*. You should be able to identify the question at the beginning of the story and give examples of how the question is being answered throughout the story.

   a. Sometimes it's only after reading a story, such as a folk tale, when you recognize that the purpose of the story was to answer a question. The question usually is about nature or why things happen the way they do. For instance, the story might be trying to explain why zebras have stripes or why the sun rises in the morning and sets at night (or what snowmen do when they come alive at night)!

6. **Life Experience**: Sometimes the narrator is simply describing an interesting experience and is not actively solving a problem. The narrative could be a real or fictional experience. Examples would be personal narratives. By the end of the story, you should be able to describe the details of the experience and who's having it.

As we continue through this book, we will be sure to pay attention to the structure of the stories we read!

In each box below, copy a passage from the book or magazine you're reading that shows the text structure of your story.

The text structure is _____ and I know this because
_____
_____

The text structure is _____ and I know this because
_____
_____

Plot, Setting and Character

Plot refers to the action in the story. It's what the **characters** do. You should be able to list the main events in the plot from beginning to end. If you list something that isn't action, then it isn't plot.

- An example of a story event that is part of a plot might be: *Mr. Johnson brought home a new puppy and gave it to his son, Pete.*

- An example of a supporting detail that is *not* part of the plot would be: *Pete felt happy when he saw the golden retriever puppy.* This is a description of feeling, not action.

A plot can be sequenced and summarized. You could summarize the plot of the story <u>Robin Hood Gets Away</u> on page 23 by saying, *Robin Hood is almost arrested for looking like an outlaw but earns his freedom back by winning an archery contest.*

Setting is the time and place where the story is happening. It could be on a distant planet two thousand years in the future, or in a child's bedroom at night. Setting can change in the story. Characters may move from one place to another, and stories can take place over hours, days, weeks, months, or even years.

On the next page, let's read Robin Hood Gets Away. You'll see how I highlighted examples of Problem and Solution narrative structure. When you're finished reading this page, turn to page 31 and read the story *Fury Mountain*. Answer the questions that follow it.

Robin Hood Gets Away

One fine day Robin Hood was looking for adventure in the forest when he met an old man dressed in poor clothes.

Robin swapped clothes with the old man, took his bow and arrow and went into town. As he was looking around, the Sheriff's men grabbed hold of him because they thought he was an outlaw.

Robin saw that there was an archery contest starting, so he told the Sheriff's men that he was just a poor old man coming to try his luck at shooting.

The soldiers laughed and let Robin go to the contest. When it was Robin's turn he put all his arrows into the bullseye. The Sheriff was surprised and gave Robin a bag of silver. "Tell me, old man, where did you learn to shoot like that?"

"A man called Robin Hood taught me," Robin replied, as he hobbled away laughing to himself.

Title

Orientation (Setting)

Beginning Event w/Plot Complications

Resolution (solution)

Ending

Fury Mountain

Most days Carrie hated when her alarm clock woke her up, but not today. Today was different.

Carrie jumped out of bed, wide awake and excited. This morning her family was going to Fury Mountain theme park. This was Carrie's first time at the amusement park and she was super excited.

"Carrie," her mother called. "Are you ready?"

"Coming!" Carrie replied.

Carrie's family piled into the car. They drove for over an hour until they were far away from the city. Once they left the city and the suburbs, there weren't many buildings to see. Instead there were trees and fields. Then, looming on the horizon, appeared the great red arc of Fury Mountain's famous roller coaster.

"Wow!" she exclaimed. "Look at that!"

"Yes," said her little brother, Will. "We're going to ride that first!"

Carrie was excited—but also scared. It looked terrifying. There were loops and twists, and she could hear the people's screams as the roller coaster cars zipped along.

After they got into the park, her brother dragged her in line for the roller coaster. Carrie tried to get away.

"What's the matter?" he asked.

"I don't think I can do it."

Will frowned. "We came all the way here. You're going to back down now?

Carrie's cheeks burned with embarrassment. She was letting her brother down, but she was so scared. Suddenly her dad came up to them and asked, "Is everything all right?"

"Carrie won't ride the roller coaster," Will complained.

"Well, maybe she'd like to go with me instead?"

Carrie nodded eagerly. She would feel braver riding next to her father.

"Problem solved!" her dad declared.

Together, they road Fury Mountain's famous roller coaster. It was thrilling, and the most exciting thing Carrie had ever done before, even though she had her eyes closed most of the time!

"That was great!" she exclaimed as they got off the ride. "Can we do it again?"

Take a yellow highlighter and mark 3 details that describe the **setting** (place and time). Take a pink highlighter and mark three examples of **plot** (action) in the story. Then answer the following questions.

1. Tell how the setting changed in the story. _____
_____

2. Is this story fantasy or realistic? _____How
do you know? _____
_____

3. What was the beginning event? _____
_____
_____

4. What was the plot complication? _____
_____
_____

5. What was the solution to the problem? _____
_____
_____

6. How did the story end? _____
_____

7. What is the text structure? _____
_____

In the box below, copy a passage from the story you're reading that describes the setting.

In the box below, write two examples of plot events happening in your story. This means two different actions the characters are taking.

1.

2.

Cause and Effect

Very often something happens in a story because of something else that came before it. The first event is the **cause**. A cause is a reason why something happened.

The next event is the **effect**, or result. An effect is something that happens or is felt because of something else.

STEPS TO FINDING THE CAUSE AND EFFECT

1. Think about what just happened in your story. This event is the effect. Something came first to cause this to happen.
2. Ask yourself, "Why did this happen?" This is the cause.
3. Clue words: because, so, as a result, therefore, due to, thus, since

---

AN EXAMPLE OF CAUSE AND EFFECT

Martha got a new train for Christmas. She played with it all day and night. The next day she was very tired.

Why was she tired? (This is the effect. You are being asked to look for the cause.)

She is tired **because** she was up all night playing with her new train. (The cause of Martha being tired was playing all night with her train)

The word "because" has the word "cause" in it. The words following "because" will tell you what caused the event or effect to happen.

Read the short story "Olivia's Concert Night." Then finish filling out the Cause and Effect graphic organizer on the next page.

~~~

Olivia's Concert Night

Olivia's foot bounced up and down as she waited for her turn to take the stage. She took long, slow breaths to calm her nerves. She closed her eyes and imagined herself playing the flute and the audience cheering for her and her classmates at the end. Tonight was the first concert for the fourth grade band and Olivia was nervous. She hoped all the weeks of practicing the flute would pay off.

When the concert began she saw her mother, father, and little brother, Alex, sitting in the front row. Alex made a goofy face at her, but Olivia ignored him. She kept her attention on the music sheet in front of her. As the music went on, she felt herself relax. Her fingers played the notes almost perfectly.

She glanced over at her mom, whose eyes were filled with proud tears. After the concert, Olivia thanked her mother for all the nights she helped her practice.

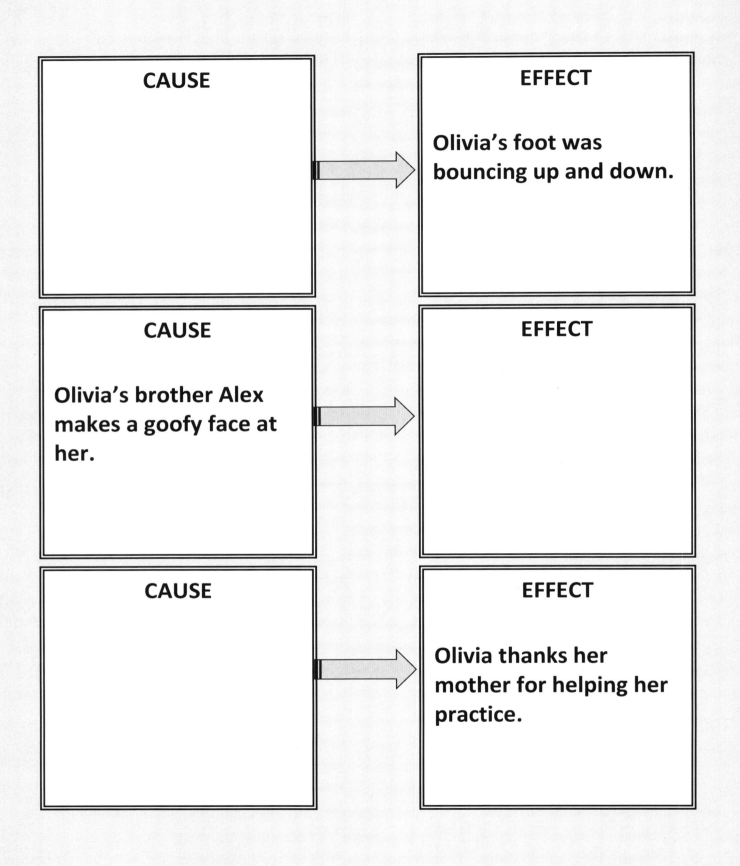

CAUSE

EFFECT

Olivia's foot was bouncing up and down.

CAUSE

Olivia's brother Alex makes a goofy face at her.

EFFECT

CAUSE

EFFECT

Olivia thanks her mother for helping her practice.

Directions: Read the story, "The Ant and Grasshopper" by Aesop. When finished, fill in the graphic organizer on page 24.

The Ant and the Grasshopper

In a field one summer's day a Grasshopper was hopping about, chirping and singing to its heart's content. An Ant passed by, carrying an ear of corn he was taking to the nest.

"Why not come and chat with me," said the Grasshopper, "instead of toiling in that way?"

"I am helping to lay up food for the winter," said the Ant, "and I recommend you do the same."

"Why bother about winter?" said the Grasshopper, "We have got plenty of food at present." But the Ant went on its way and continued its toil. When the winter came the Grasshopper had no food and found itself dying of hunger. But the ants were passing out corn and grain from the stores they had collected in the summer. They had plenty to eat, and the Grasshopper felt very sorry. That's when the Grasshopper knew:

It is best to prepare for the days of necessity.

Directions: Look back in the text. Highlight three causes in yellow and their effects in orange, then fill in the graphic organizer. The first one has been done for you.

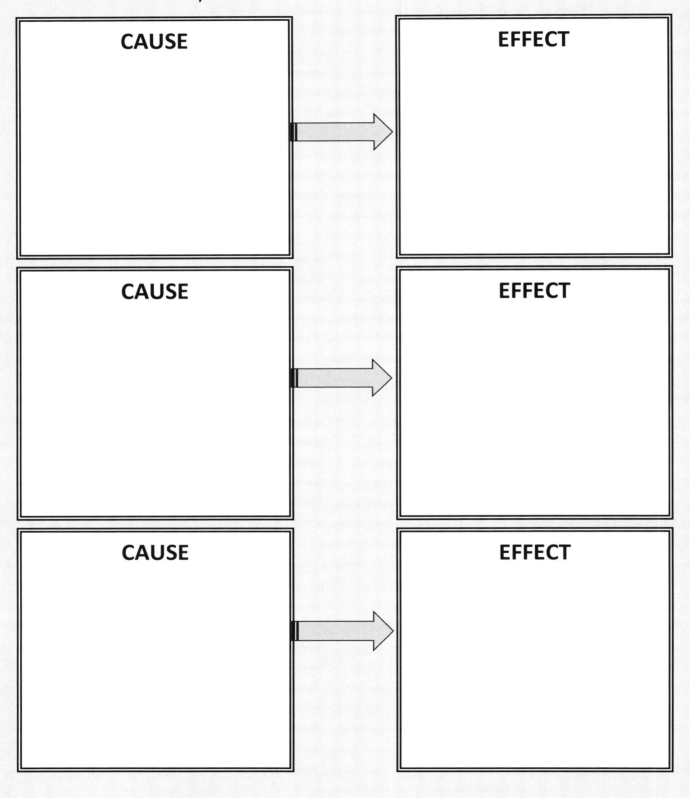

CAUSE	EFFECT
CAUSE	EFFECT
CAUSE	EFFECT

INDEPENDENT WORK—Cause and Effect

Directions: Fill in three cause and effect examples from the story or novel you're reading.

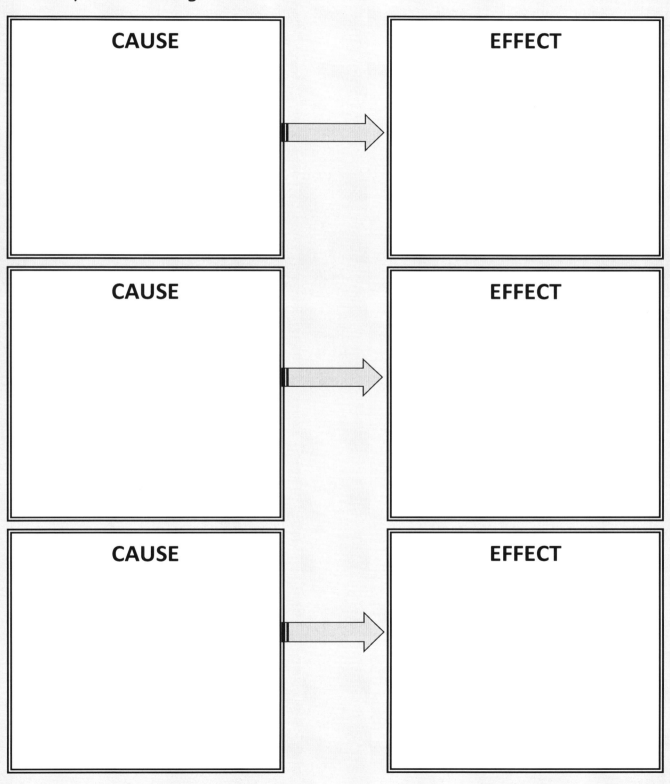

CAUSE

EFFECT

CAUSE

EFFECT

CAUSE

EFFECT

Sequence of Events

Like an Oreo cookie, most stories have a beginning, middle, and end. **Sequence** is the order in which things happen during the story.

There are questions we can ask ourselves about the order of events. "Did this event happen before this event?" "Did it happen after?" "Did it happen at the same time?" "Did this event happen first?" "Last?" "Right before this event?" "Right after this event?"

It's a good idea to go back and re-read the passage to be sure.

We have already studied cause and effect. When listing a sequence of events in a story, we are listing a chain of cause and effect events. These are the important events that drive the plot of the story to the conclusion.

Some clue words that show sequence:
first, then, last, before, after, finally, next, later

Clue words used when things are happening at the same time:
while, as, during, meanwhile

More sequence clue words—Clock Times, Years and Dates:
7:30 am, 1963, 6:00 pm, 876 BC, six o'clock in the morning, 1/28/72, two hours before, April 11, 2007, several hours later, five years ago 12:00 midnight, many years later

Still more clue words:
Days of the week, months, seasons, morning, noon, evening

Let's read the following story. After, we'll finish filling in the graphic organizer on page 44 with the main events of the story.

Night of the Storm

Alex awoke with a start. He shivered under his blanket as he listened to the fierce wind thump and pound his house. The crackling lightning lit up his dark bedroom. Rain fell in torrents outside. Alex worried that all the rain would collapse the roof.

Suddenly the thunder roared so loudly it shook the whole house. He let out a little cry.

A few seconds later, his father came into the room. "Everything all right in here?" he asked gently.

"I'm fine," Alex answered in a shaky voice.

His father sat down on the edge of Alex's bed. "The storm is only a bunch of noise," he explained. "Nothing that can hurt you."

"I know," Alex said, trying to sound brave. He rolled over and closed his eyes. "Good night."

His father patted his shoulder and left the room.

Alex fell into a deep sleep and had the scariest dream of his life. He dreamt that the raging storm had punched a hole in the roof, and his house was flooding with rain water. Rising water lifted his bed and swept him out of his room.

Outside, all the cars and houses on his street were gone. Everything was underwater. He rode the rapids until it took him to the edge of a tall waterfall. At the bottom lay a churning, frothing darkness. Alex opened his mouth to scream when …

… strong hands started to shake him. Alex opened his eyes and looked around. The storm was over, and the sun was shining. It was morning!

"What happened?" he asked, rubbing his eyes.

"You were dreaming," his father said, smiling.

~~~

As you can see, there are many events in this story. Some events are very important to note because they *caused* something else to happen. Other actions are not as important, but they are included because they're descriptive. In other words, they help bring the story to life.

For example, the fact Alex is shivering under his blanket is not that important, but it's what a kid does when he's scared or cold. The fact there's a storm is important because it makes Alex cry out, which brings his father into his room.

The storm, you see, sets the story in motion. The storm—and Alex's fear of it—*causes* the nightmare. The nightmare brings his father back into the room to wake him up. These are main events in the cause-and-effect chain that we want to pay careful attention to.

Finish filling out the graphic organizer on the next page.

Vocabulary Review

~~~

synonym
fiction
narrative
realistic
fantasy
text structure
plot
setting
cause/effect
sequence
visualize
inference
trait
figurative
language
theme
main idea
summarize

BEGINNING

(include the setting)

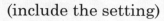

In the beginning, Alex is sleeping in bed when he's woken up in the middle of the night by a loud thunderstorm outside.

MIDDLE

Next,

Then, his father assures Alex that the storm can't hurt him, so Alex falls back to sleep.

After,

END

In the end, Alex thinks he's going to go over a water fall in his bed, but his father wakes him up and tells him he was just dreaming.

Directions: Read this excerpt and sequence the main events on the next page. Then answer the comprehension questions on page 32.

Excerpt from <u>Animal Quest 5: Land of Ice</u> by David R. Smith

A group of four men and two women, lugging ropes, harnesses, and other equipment, followed Professor Feathers out into the frigid Antarctic night.

The owl took to flight to search for the children. The moon was full, and in its light the icy snow gleamed. He saw no sign of Olivia or Alex, however.

I may be too late, he feared. *What if the crevasse is already covered up again in fresh snow?*

The Great Horned Owl decided this was no time for *what-ifs.* Such thinking was useless at a time like this.

He used his sharp vision and keen hearing to try to detect the children. A moment later, he saw a jagged dark line in the ice below.

A crevasse!

His heart jolting, Professor Feathers dived straight for it.

"The owl sees something!" one of the men called from the ground below. Floodlights were turned on and their beams focused on the crevasse.

Without a moment to lose, Professor Feathers soared straight down into the hole in the broken ice. The crevasse was narrow, with jagged pieces of ice sticking out of the sides. Twice Professor Feathers clipped his wing on the ice, causing a stabbing pain to shoot through his body.

At the bottom of the crevasse he found Olivia and Alex. They were wedged in the ice. If not for the owl's excellent vision, the children would have been impossible to detect down here. They were so far down, even their cries would have gone unheard.

BEGINNING

(include the setting)

In the beginning,

MIDDLE

Next,

Then,

After,

END

In the end,

Comprehension Check

1. Take a highlighter and mark 3 details that describe the **setting** (place and time) in <u>Animal Quest 5: Land of Ice.</u>

2. Who is the main character, or *protagonist*, in this story?_____
    _____

3. Is this story fantasy or realistic? _____How do you know? _____
    _____

4. What is the text structure of this story?
    a. Problem and solution
    b. Circular text
    c. Framing-Question
    d. Diary

5. List one cause and its effect from this story: _____
    _____
    _____

Making Inferences

An author will not tell us everything about the characters or plot. Authors want us to figure some things out for ourselves. We can do this by making educated guesses. We call these guesses "inferences."

To make an inference about a text, you need two things; background knowledge and evidence from the text.

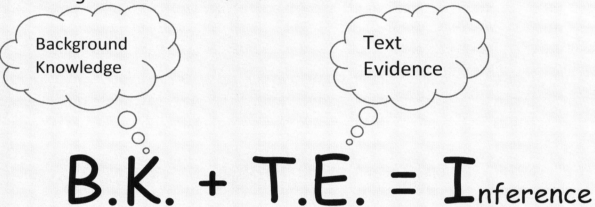

B.K. + T.E. = Inference

Activity: Use your background knowledge and text evidence to answer this question: *Why is Sami in trouble?*

> *Sami rushed into the classroom, threw her backpack in the coat closet, and hurried to her seat, just after the morning bell rang. As Sami took her seat, Mrs. Polimeni sighed, and said, "Young lady, you're in trouble!"*

You did it! You made an inference. Not so hard, right? On the next page, let's read another story and make some inferences!

The Field Trip

The day was finally here. Sara checked her backpack for the third time to make sure she had everything she needed for the field trip: a notebook, two pencils, her permission slip, and a camera. She wouldn't want to miss the opportunity to take pictures of the tigers, crocodiles, or polar bears. She especially loved watching the silly monkeys play in their cages. When it was time to board the bus, she eagerly sat in the front seat. She wanted to be the first one off the bus.

Where is Sara going on the field trip?_____

What background knowledge and text clues helped you know this?

Background Knowledge	Text Evidence

How does Sara feel about going on the field trip? _____

Background Knowledge	Text Evidence

<u>Directions: Read the two Harry Potter excerpts and answer the questions.</u>

Excerpt from *Harry Potter and the Sorcerer's Stone*
By J.K. Rowling

Nearly ten years had passed since the Dursleys had woken up to find their nephew on the front step, but Privet Drive had hardly changed at all. The sun rose on the same tidy front gardens and lit up the brass number four on the Dursleys' front door; it crept into their living room, which was almost exactly the same as it had been on the night when Mr. Dursley had seen that fateful news report about the owls. Only the photographs on the mantelpiece really showed how much time had passed. Ten years ago, there had been lots of pictures of what looked like a large pink beach ball wearing different-colored bonnets - but Dudley Dursley was no longer a baby, and now the photographs showed a large blond boy riding his first bicycle, on a carousel at the fair, playing a computer game with his father, being hugged and kissed by his mother. The room held no sign at all that another boy lived in the house, too.

How do the Dursleys feel about their son Dudley?_____

What background knowledge and text clues helped you know this?

Background Knowledge	Text Evidence

Excerpt from *Harry Potter and the Sorcerer's Stone*, cont'd
By J.K. Rowling

Yet Harry Potter was still there, asleep at the moment, but not for long. His Aunt Petunia was awake and it was her shrill voice that made the first noise of the day.

"Up! Get up! Now!"

Harry woke with a start. His aunt rapped on the door again.

"Up!" she screeched. Harry heard her walking toward the kitchen and then the sound of the frying pan being put on the stove. He rolled onto his back and tried to remember the dream he had been having. It had been a good one. There had been a flying motorcycle in it. He had a funny feeling he'd had the same dream before.

His aunt was back outside the door.

"Are you up yet?" she demanded.

"Nearly," said Harry.

"Well, get a move on, I want you to look after the bacon. And don't you dare let it burn, I want everything perfect on Dudley's birthday."

How do the Dursleys feel about Harry Potter? _____

Background Knowledge	Text Evidence

Character Traits

In the last chapter we learned about inferences. We make inferences based on our background knowledge and what's written in the text. We can also figure out a character's traits by the things they do or say.

A trait is a quality that a character has. Qualities are usually consistent in a story. If your story's protagonist is helpful to others in chapter one, most likely your protagonist will be helpful to others at the end.

Writers will also share with us how characters are feeling at different times. Feelings are *not* the same as traits.

Vocabulary Review

synonym
fiction
narrative
realistic
fantasy
text structure
plot
setting
cause/effect
sequence
visualize
inference
trait
figurative language
theme
main idea
summarize

Think about Sara in *The Field Trip*. We know Sara feels excited for the trip. Sitting in the front seat of the bus eagerly. Packing a camera to take pictures. These are things that people do before they have an exciting experience.

Feelings are usually temporary. Character traits, however, are consistent, and they control how a character acts throughout a story. Characters will act consistently AND predictably most of the time.

What can we infer is one of Sara's character traits? If you're not sure, look at the list on the next page. Be sure to read the definitions.

Character Traits

- **Alert** – Being aware of what is going on around you, so you can make the right decisions.

- **Benevolent** – Giving to others without thinking of yourself.

- **Cautious** – Timing things just right to accomplish right actions.

- **Compassionate** – Doing what it takes to help others feel better.

- **Confident** – Doing what is best without second guessing.

- **Creative** – Approaching a need, a task, or an idea from a new perspective.

- **Deceptive** – Doesn't tell the truth; tries to trick people.

- **Decisive** – Recognizing what needs to be done and then doing it.

- **Dependable** – Doing what you said you'd do, no matter the challenges.

- **Determined** – Trying to accomplish right goals at the right time, no matter who or what tries to stop you.

- **Earnest** – Serious about reaching a goal.

- **Enthusiastic** – Expressing joy in a task or event.

- **Faithful** – Believing that acting with good character pays off in the end.

- **Flexible** – Willingness to change plans or ideas.

- **Forgiving** – Not holding a grudge.

- **Friendly** – Cheerfully sharing food, shelter, or conversation to help others.

- **Generous** – Thoughtfully giving to those in need.

- **Gentle** – Showing consideration and personal concern for others.

- **Grateful** – Letting others know their positive actions meant something to you.
- **Humble** – Recognizing you can't be successful without others helping you.
- **Ingenious** – Acting smartly and doing what needs to be done.
- **Joyful** – Keeping a good attitude, even in tough times.
- **Loyal** – Using difficult times to demonstrate commitment to those you serve.
- **Miserable**—Having a bad attitude and failing to see the positive side of things.
- **Obedient** – Quickly and cheerfully carrying out the direction of those who are responsible for you.
- **Patient** – Waiting out a difficult situation.
- **Persuasive** – Using intelligent reasoning to convince others to see things your way.
- **Resourceful** – Finding practical uses for things others would overlook.
- **Responsible** – Knowing and doing what is expected of you.
- **Sincerity** – Eagerness to do what is right for unselfish reasons.
- **Spiteful** – Acting envious or jealous of others.
- **Studious** – One who takes studying and learning seriously.
- **Truthfulness** – Earning future trust by accurately telling facts.
- **Wicked** – Having a mean spirit, wishing to do harm to others.
- **Wise** – Having great knowledge and insight

Directions: Let's talk about Sara again. You just picked a character trait (or two) that describes her. Traits are consistent qualities of a character throughout a story. Keeping Sara's trait(s) in mind, let's write an ending to her story. What happens during her field trip to the zoo? For example, if she's "enthusiastic," then she should act enthusiastically! Write your story on the lines below.

The Field Trip

The day was finally here. Sara checked her backpack for the third time to make sure she had everything she needed for the field trip: a notebook, two pencils, her permission slip, and a camera. She wouldn't want to miss the opportunity to take pictures of the tigers, crocodiles, or polar bears. She especially loved watching the silly monkeys play in their cages. When it was time to board the bus, she eagerly sat in the front seat. She wanted to be the first one off the bus.

_____

_____

_____

_____

_____

_____

_____

_____

_____

In the box below, write an excerpt from the story you're reading that shows your main character's traits.

A character trait of _____ is _____.

What background knowledge and text clues helped you know this?

Background Knowledge	Text Evidence

Making Predictions

A **prediction** is thinking about what the story, passage, or book will be about. It is also thinking about what will happen next.

Before Reading:
1. Read the title, look at the picture on the cover closely, and predict what the story will be about.
2. Many times, you can read a summary of the book on the back cover and it will give you a sense of what it is about.

During and After Reading:
1. Think about what has happened so far.
2. Think about the clues that will help you figure out what will happen next.
3. Think about your own experience (things you know from your own life) or prior knowledge. This will help you make an **inference**.
4. Make a prediction and give evidence to prove it. Use clues from the story and/or your own experience to prove it.

Good readers make predictions naturally all the time. Taking the time to stop and make a prediction while reading gives your brain a chance to catch up and understand better what you've just read.

Remember: Reading is not a race ... it's an experience!

Directions: Read the story Amy's Halloween Secret. Answer each of the prediction questions before you read on!

Annabelle's Halloween Secret

It was almost October 31, and Annabelle was excited. Halloween was her favorite day of the year. It was better than Christmas, because she got so many more presents … in the form of candy!

Annabelle was also excited because she had just moved to Brooklyn in New York City. Her father had been given a promotion at his job, so Annabelle, her mom, and her dad had packed up their things in Dayton, Ohio, and moved their lives to the East Coast.

Annabelle didn't know much about New York City. She wondered what Halloween in Brooklyn was like. Did the kids dress up and go trick or treating, like they did in Dayton? Did parents hand out candy, or did they only have healthy treats? What kind of costumes did people wear? Annabelle was impatient to find out; thank goodness it was already October 29!

Make a prediction:

What do you think Halloween might be like in New York City?

_____

_____

On the 31st, Annabelle rushed home from school, and found her costume laid out on her bed, all ready to wear. Her mom had stayed up late the night before working on it. Now it was ready, and it looked perfect! Annabelle loved the Winnie the Pooh stories, and this year, she was going to be Tigger, the bouncy, happy tiger. Her mom had found the perfect orange and black fabric for her costume, which also matched with the orange and black colors of Halloween.

After Annabelle's mom had painted whiskers on Annabelle's face, the two of them set off to explore the neighborhood. Annabelle's mom had cleverly sewn a pouch into the Tigger costume, where Annabelle could store her candy. They went around her block and then ended up near a park, where a lot of kids were playing in their Halloween costumes. A small house stood at the center of the park. Annabelle wanted to go closer and investigate. A plaque next to the house said this was the "Old Stone House," built in 1699.

"That's more than three hundred years ago!" Annabelle said to her mother. "Does anyone live there now?"

"It's Halloween," her mother said. "I think we should knock on the door and find out."

Make a prediction:

What do you think Annabelle will discover in the house? _____

_____

_____

Annabelle was a little nervous, so she held onto her mother's hand as they walked up to the door. They knocked. No response. Annabelle tried again, this time more loudly. She thought she heard voices inside. Children's voices?

Annabelle tried pushing the door open and was startled when it moved! Why wasn't the house locked? Who was inside it? Still clutching her mother's hand, Annabelle began exploring. "Hello?" she called out. "Anybody home?"

Silence.

"Trick or treat?" she tried.

Annabelle and her mother walked all around the house, upstairs and downstairs. It was dark, and there were no light switches. It was hard to make out much detail, but Annabelle could imagine that a family had lived there three hundred years before. There was clearly no candy to be had, so they decided to leave. Right as Annabelle was shutting the door, she thought she saw a little girl, very pale, run past her in the living room. "Come back soon!" the girl whispered to Annabelle, which gave Annabelle the chills.

"What's wrong?" her mother asked her.

"Oh, nothing," Annabelle said. She decided that the ghost girl in the Old Stone House would be her Halloween secret.

Confirm your predictions: Were your two predictions correct? Why or why not? _____

_____

1. Was this story fantasy or realistic? _____

2. What is the text structure of Annabelle's Halloween Secret?

   (Review pages 26-27 if you're not sure) _____

3. What is the setting of this story? _____

Sequence the events in the story.

   a. In the beginning, _____

   _____

   b. Next, _____

   _____

   c. Then, _____

   _____

   d. After, _____

   _____

   e. Finally, _____

   _____

4. What is a character trait that you think best describes Annabelle

   and why? _____

   _____

   _____

Figurative Language

Authors don't always say what they mean. Why, you ask? Probably because it would be boring if they did.

Narrative writers want us to see a "mind movie." In other words, they want us to see pictures in our mind of the action. We'll call those pictures "figures" from now on. If a writer does her job right, we should very clearly see the figures that the author is describing.

Consider these two sentences:

The boy was very mad.

or

The boy had smoke coming out of his ears.

Which description is more entertaining and easier to imagine? Exactly. The first sentence doesn't describe a figure at all. It just tells us that a boy is mad. The second example, however, *shows* us an angry boy by describing smoke coming out of his ears, like it does from a hot kettle. People who are mad are said to be "hot," so it makes sense to write this figurative sentence. This is also an example of **hyperbole**.

There are many examples of figurative language that we find in books.

SIMILE – A simile describes one thing by comparing it to another thing using the words like, as, or than.
   Example – The rain poured down like a waterfall.
   Meaning: The rain coming down was like a waterfall, so it was
          coming down fast and hard.

METAPHOR – A metaphor is a comparison in which a writer says that someone or something *is* something else.

      Example – My baby brother is a little monkey.

      Meaning: The little boy is being compared to a monkey because he can't sit still and behave, just like a monkey.

PERSONIFICATION – Personification is when a non-living thing is described as having human-like qualities.

      Example – The trees waved at us.

      Meaning – Tress, of course, can't actually wave to us. However, since the wind is pushing the branches back and forth, they look like they're waving at us.

IDIOM – An idiom is a phrase whose words don't mean what they actually say.

      Example – It's raining cats and dogs.

      Meaning – The phrase "raining cats and dogs" does not mean cats and dogs are falling from the sky. It means it is raining very hard.

HYPERBOLE – Hyperbole is a big exaggeration that is not meant to be taken seriously.

      Example – I'm so hungry, I could eat a horse.

      Meaning – Although no one can eat an entire horse, you must be *very* hungry if you're even thinking about it!

Choose a word from the box that matches each example of figurative language. Then read Hansel and Gretel and answer the questions.

| simile   metaphor   personification   idiom   hyperbole |

1. Mom said we can stay up late to watch the movie, and the icing on the cake is she'll make us popcorn, too! _____

2. She laughs like a hyena at all my jokes. _____

3. Jim's stomach begs him for food all the time. _____

4. I think my teacher is a walking dictionary. _____

5. Her new shoes were killing her feet! _____

6. "You can tell me anything," he said. "I'm all ears." _____

7. I thought the test was a piece of cake! _____

BONUS!!

Choose two sentences from the list above and illustrate them below!

Hansel and Gretel

Once there was an old woodcutter who lived with his wife and two children, Hansel and Gretel. They were so poor that some days they had nothing to eat. The woodcutter's wife was a mean, spiteful woman. She grew to despise her two children and their constantly complaining stomachs. Her own stomach, in fact, growled at her daily like a caged animal.

"We need to do something about them kids!" she snarled at her husband one night as they sat in their rockers by the fire.

"Do something?" The man looked at her in alarm. "Like what?"

The woman leaned over so the children, who were upstairs in the loft, wouldn't overhear. "Get rid of 'em once and for all," she whispered. "They're eating us out of house and home! If it was just the two of us, why, we'd want for nothin'."

The old man stared into the fire for a long time before speaking. "There's darkness in your heart, old woman," he finally said.

"Aye, maybe," she answered with a cackle, "but at least there'd be more food in my belly!"

The old woman was right to be worried about her two children eavesdropping. Both overheard the terrible plan and the unfortunate end waiting for them. And they both heard their father agree to it. They loved their father and he loved them back; but he was a weak man controlled by their vicious mother.

"What are we going to do?" Gretel asked Hansel.

STOP! Write a prediction of what will happen next.

"Don't worry," he said. "I'll get you out of here."

As soon as they heard their mother and father go to bed and their buzz-saw snores fill the tiny cabin, Hansel and Gretel snuck out the front door. They each carried nothing more than rucksacks with a few supplies and a couple scraps of bread crust. They would not be going home again.

Dawn was still hours away and the forest was cold and dark. The sounds of wolves howling back and forth to each other filled every corner of the wooded land. Every snapping twig made the anxious children jump. A pointy branch snatched at Gretel's coat, and she shrieked and batted her hands at it like she was fighting off an enemy.

"It's okay," Hansel told his frightened little sister. "The next town isn't far away." But he had no idea when they'd come to the next town.

In a little while the forest thinned and opened into a clearing. To their amazement, they saw a small cottage gleaming in the full moon light. What made it gleam was the candy covering its walls and roof. The house seemed to be made from peppermint sticks, chocolate bars, gum drops, licorice, and marshmallows. The children dropped their rucksacks and ran to the cottage. They greedily started ripping pieces of candy off the house and shoving it into their hungry mouths. When they'd eaten their fill, they sat on the porch to rest. It hadn't occurred to either of them that somebody might live there.

They wouldn't have long to wonder, however. The front door opened on squeaky hinges. The shadow of a tall figure spilled onto the porch. "Who goes there?" a harsh voice rumbled from the shadows. The voice of an ancient sounding woman.

STOP! Write another prediction of what will happen next.

Hansel answered for both he and his sister. "We're Hansel and Gretel. We were making our way through the woods when we spied your house in the clearing."

"I see," the old woman said slowly. "Two children alone in the woods at night." She took a step closer into the moonlight. Hansel gasped. The old woman had a hooked nose and a pointy chin. Bumpy warts speckled her long face. Her eyes shone in the dark like two silver dollars. "And very hungry children, by the sight of you."

Gretel waved her marshmallow-sticky hands at the stranger.

"Well, come in, then," the old lady offered, swinging the door open wide. The smell of freshly baked bread and bubbling stew wafted out.

Hansel and Gretel knew it was wrong to accept an invitation like this from a stranger. They knew strangers could be dangerous—didn't Ma beat that sense into them more than once? But they were children, and children are led by their noses, stomachs, and curiosity. And those are powerfully hard senses to ignore.

The children stayed not one or two but three weeks, feasting on the most delicious food they'd ever tasted. It was almost *bewitching* how good and plentiful everything was—the loaves of bread, platters of meats and boats of gravy, bushels of fruit and the endless supply of candy. Not once did they actually see the old woman cook anything, however. It just sort of appeared, like figments of a dream, right before their eyes and on their plates. And so they ate, and they ate, and they ate until…

They became so fat you could roll them like cannonballs.

One night the old lady, who called herself Amerial, stood over Hansel and Gretel approvingly while they shoveled mashed potatoes, sweet corn, and slabs of roast beef down their throats. And candy, of course. Lots and lots of candy.

"My, my. I think it's time," Amerial said, scratching the whisker on her chin.

"Time for what?" asked Hansel, wiping his greasy mouth.

"For my dinner!" Amerial fetched up Hansel and carried him as if he were light as a feather over to her cooking stove. She opened the stove door and tried to shove him inside, but he wouldn't fit. Truth be told, Hansel had gained so much weight that his blubbery head and neck wouldn't fit through the opening.

"Hey, you stop that!" Gretel rushed over and smacked the witch (for surely only a witch would've had the strength to carry Hansel like that.) Amerial dropped Hansel, who struck the floor like a sack of chicken feed, and chased Gretel around the cottage. Hansel tripped the witch as she ran by, and the wicked old woman fell into the blazing hot stove! Hansel slammed the door shut and locked it.

Hansel and Gretel stared at the amazing cottage of candy all around them. They couldn't believe their luck. When they left their home behind, Hansel had no idea what to expect. He thought they'd be wandering the woods, hungry, for days or even weeks before finding somebody to help them. But right now … things were really cooking for them!

QUESTIONS FOR DISCUSSION:

Which traits best describe Hansel, Gretel, and Amerial? Why?

Can you think of another way Hansel and Gretel might have escaped the witch?

Re-read Hansel and Gretel. Then answer the questions below.

1. Write a sentence from paragraph 1 that contains a simile. _____

    _____

    _____

2. "They became so fat you could roll them like cannonballs" is an

    example of _____

3. Write an example of an idiom from paragraph 4. _____

    _____

    _____

Directions: In the box below, write a sentence containing figurative language from the book you're reading. Say what type of figurative language it is.

Type of figurative language _____

Theme and Main Idea

Authors have something to say when they write. They are writing to entertain us with a story, but they usually have a **theme**.

According to the Oxford English Dictionary's definition, theme is "the subject of a piece of writing."

The subject can often be said in one or two words. You might read something and say, "This story is about kindness." Okay, but you might get asked to explain the "author's message" about kindness, or what the "lesson" or "main idea" of the story is all about.

If this confuses you, you're not alone. Theme is vague, or unclear. The author never just tells you what it's all about (unless he or she is writing a fable or some other type of folk tale for the single reason of teaching you a lesson). Authors expect you to think for yourself and have some fun figuring out the theme!

But it isn't easy, so let's start simplifying things a bit.

Think of a story like a train carrying you and your main character through the plot. The train moves forward, from the beginning, through the middle, and to the end. Yet there are many ways to get from one place to another. The path the author chooses to take you is the *theme*.

In other words, theme is the track on which the train moves. Nobody thinks about the track while they're riding on a train. They look out the window and watch the pretty scenery go by. As we read scenes in a book or story, however, the author is showing us these events for a reason. The reason is the theme. And, in the end, the *purpose* of the journey for you and the protagonist should become clear.

So, again, what is theme? *It's the deeper layer of meaning running beneath a story's surface.*

Let's read about a boy named Ron.

> Ron is lonely. He has no friends when he moves to a new school. After a week of being nice to everyone and trying to fit in, Ron is invited to a birthday party! He goes and meets lots of new kids and makes lots of new friends. In the end, Ron is a happy boy in his new school.

What is the subject, or theme, of this simple little story that I've shared with you? Do you think the subject might be "friendship?" Okay, it's a start. But I want you to think a little deeper now.

What do you suppose the author wants you to think about "friendship"? What are you *feeling* about friendship after reading this story? Is making friends a good thing? Now we're getting somewhere.

Ron seems to be feeling good at the end of the story. He's a "happy boy" after he meets "lots of new kids and makes lots of new friends."

What's the theme then?

We need to use the skill of inferencing now. Background knowledge plus text evidence equals an inference, right? What can we *infer* is the message, or theme, of this story?

First, you know you feel better when you have friends to play with. In the text, Ron is a "happy boy" (effect) after he made "lots of new friends." (cause)

Maybe we could say the theme is, "Making new friends can make us feel happy" or "Life is happier when we have friends." Both of these themes make sense because of what happened in the story.

Let's review what we've learned so far.

- Authors write stories to entertain us but also to communicate a deeper message about life.
- The deeper message is called a theme, or sometimes a "message" or a "lesson."
- Theme is very tricky to capture in just a sentence, but it can be done. Often, there can be more than one theme!
- You need to make an inference to figure out the theme.
- And perhaps the most important point to remember is: **You must back up what you say the theme is with details from the story.**

(Why, you ask, is this last point so important? Simply, when the author wrote the story, he could have chosen 1,000,000 different directions for his story to take. He didn't; he chose *these* events. The events tell the story of the protagonist and serve the purpose of the novel, so we *must* pay attention to details to fully understand what the novel's deeper meaning is.)

Here, then, is one final definition of theme...
Theme is the deeper layer of meaning running beneath the story's surface. While the surface story entertains us, the theme helps us to reach a deeper understanding of the human condition.

Pretty cool, isn't it?

> HUMAN CONDITION—THE KEY EVENTS, EMOTIONS, AND TRAITS THAT MAKE UP HUMAN LIFE.

The **main idea** is what the paragraph or whole story is mostly about. The main idea can and should be stated in one short sentence. The **details** tell more about the main idea. They show us what the characters are doing and how they're reacting to events in the plot. The details are very important to pay attention to.

Steps to finding the Main Idea:

1. Think about what the paragraph or story is mostly about. What is the subject? What is the theme? Now how is the author showing us the theme? This is the main idea.

2. Ask yourself, "Can I find 2 or more details that support what I think is the theme and main idea?"

I think of main idea like this: **It is the theme in *action*.** Or, to put it another way, if you think the subject of a story is "friendship" then your characters should be doing friendly things. What happens after they do friendly things? How are the characters affected? This is what the author wants you to know about friendships.

Let's hang out with Ron again. Here is his story one more time:

> Ron is lonely. He has no friends when he moves to a new school. After a week of being nice to everyone and trying to fit in, Ron is invited to a birthday party! He goes and meets lots of new kids and makes lots of new friends. In the end, Ron is a happy boy in his new school.

Okay, let's get started. Let's review what we thought the subject of the story is: **Friendship.**

Here is the theme we decided on: **Making new friends can make us feel happy.**

Now for the main idea statement. This statement must include our main character, Ron, and what he does in the story (Remember: main idea is *theme in action*). It will say something about how Ron is trying to make new friends. Why? Because this fits the subject and the theme.

> # Main Idea is
> # Theme in Action!

So, our main idea statement is: **This story is about Ron, a new boy in school, who is trying to make new friends.**

There it is. We don't have to say anything else. We're not writing a sequence of events, and we're not summarizing the whole story. (Summarizing comes in the next chapter, lucky you).

Before we proceed to summarizing, let's read a story about Barney the barn cat. When you are done, see if you can identify the subject, theme, and main idea.

Barney the Barn Cat

Barney was a large grey and white cat who lived in a barn on a farm. Barney liked living in the barn. It was warm in the winter and cool in the summer. There were many mice for Barney to chase. Best of all, Barney had a soft place to sleep in the corner of the barn.

One day Barney woke up to the sound of a dog barking. Barney peeked out from his cozy bed of straw and saw a large, slobbery dog lumbering around his barn. The dog ran in and out of the barn several times, as if it were looking for something.

What is that filthy animal doing here? wondered Barney. Barney watched as the dog nosed around everything. *What is he looking for?*

Barney felt a tingle of fear. *I hope he isn't looking for me!*

When the dog left, Barney had a meeting with the mice. The mice weren't exactly fond of Barney, but when the barn cat calls a meeting, you show up if you know what's good for you. "I want to know what that mongrel was doing in my barn!" hissed Barney.

The mice put their heads together and talked it over. "We don't know," one of them told Barney. "We've never seen that dog before."

Barney was not happy with that answer. "If you mice don't help me get rid of that dog, you will be sorry!"

"Perhaps," said the brave little mouse, "we could work out a deal."

"A deal?"

"Yes. If we help you keep the dog out of the barn, you have to promise not to chase us anymore."

Barney the barn cat didn't like making deals with mice, but he agreed.

The mice scampered off and came up with a plan. Barney watched closely as they gathered a dirty old white sheet and some sticks. They hid themselves in a dark corner of the barn, waiting. Barney waited too, curled up in his bed, trying not to shiver. He didn't want the mice to see how scared he was.

After a while the dog came back. It ran in, barked twice to announce itself, and then started to give the barn a good sniffing.

That's when the mice sprang into action.

First, they rattled the sticks and made a curious little noise that got the dog's attention. The dog turned its head and stared. Next, the white sheet slowly rose into the air. It shook a little, like a ghost, and the mice chorused a few "oohs" and a few "boos." The dog was clearly spooked. It barked fiercely at the strange thing wavering in the corner. Barney crept up behind it and swatted it on the tail! The dog yipped and yapped and bolted out of the barn, its tail between its legs.

Barney and the mice never saw the dog again, and life returned to normal. Except for one little change.

The mice didn't have to worry about Barney the barn cat chasing them anymore.

1. SUBJECT: _____

2. THEME: _____

3. MAIN IDEA: _____

_____

4. Was this story fantasy or realistic? _____ How do you know? _____

_____

5. What was the text structure of this story? _____

6. Make a prediction: What will life in the barn be like now that Barney and the mice get along? _____

_____

7. Write one Cause and one Effect from this story.

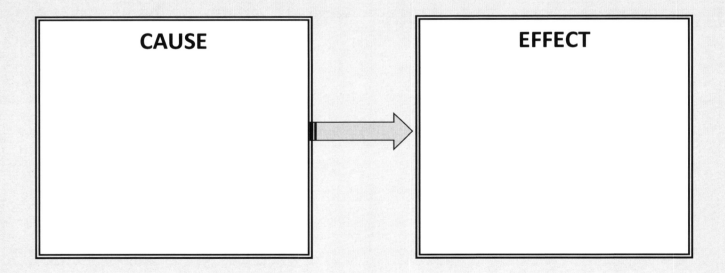

The Witch of Nightville

Princess Luna lived with her family in a sparkling castle high above the tiny hamlet of Nightville. Luna was the younger of two sisters, and at fourteen, also the most disobedient. She was a petty girl, who spent long hours staring at her plain face in the palace mirror, and daydreaming about love, glory, and riches. She was also bitterly jealous of her older sister, the lovely and graceful Princess Olivia, who was due to be wed in a fortnight.

One evening Luna stood outside her sister's bedchamber. She listened as her mother told Olivia about the upcoming wedding.

"It will be so *lovely*," boasted the Queen. "Thousands of roses, dahlias, and hydrangeas will transform our courtyard into the garden of Eden. The finest minstrels and musicians from all over the land will entertain us. All the kings and queens from the Seven Kingdoms will be in attendance, and your stunning beauty will mesmerize them."

When Luna heard this, her rage—well-known around the kingdom—boiled.

She stormed away and returned to her own bedchamber. She spent the rest of the evening plotting her revenge.

Since the early days, Luna's mother and father clearly favored Olivia. Olivia had the sort of beauty that stopped conversation when she walked into a room. Her eyes sparkled like sapphires and her smile made strangers forget what they were going to say. By contrast, Luna was a forgettable sort of pretty. With her smatter of freckles, brown eyes, and intensely shy personality, she was easy to overlook. No matter how many Latin texts she learned to read or stallions she learned to ride, Luna failed to impress her royal parents. Their lives revolved around Olivia. Nothing would ever change that fact.

About an hour later she heard a knock at her door. "May I come in?" asked Olivia.

"What do you want?" grumbled Luna.

"I came to see if you were all right," she said. "Ever since I announced my marriage plans to Prince Randolph, you've been so distant around me. I want you to be happy, that is all."

Luna rolled over in her bed and glared at her. "You really want to make me happy?"

Her sister nodded. "More than anything!"

"Then you'll get out and leave me alone forever. You think you're so special, marrying a prince and all, but you'll see. Someday, very soon, I'll be the one everyone is talking about. My beauty will light up this world and no one will forget who I am!"

"One day, Luna, you will find the prince of your dreams, too."

Luna scoffed. "He will probably be a toad of a man and his castle half the size of Randolph's."

Princess Olivia looked stricken. "I'm sorry you feel that way," she said quietly, closing the door. *Yes, you will be sorry*, thought Luna.

After night dropped its cloak over the world and the sky bloomed with stars, Luna approached the Outer Gate. She ordered the startled guards—who rarely heard the demure princess speak—to lower the gate and fetch her horse. She was sure the answer to all her problems would be found in the Forest of Magic. And she would do whatever it took to convince the witch who lived there to help her.

Princess Luna spurred her horse and it took off like a shot into the forest. After several minutes of hard riding through the near pitch-black woods, she paused to let the horse rest. All around her she heard the flutter of bats and the whine of insects in her ears. With no light from above but the cold glimmer of stars, Luna could barely see her hands in front of her face.

Suddenly, her heartbeat spiked when she heard what sounded like singing coming from up ahead. Only it wasn't a tune that a traveling minstrel might sing; it was the screechy voice of the old crone Mystia, who resided in the heart of the forest.

As Luna came closer to the singing, she stopped and dismounted. Through the thickets, Luna spied the witch hunched over a cooking fire, a wooden spoon held inches from her mouth, about to taste the broth. But the old woman didn't move; she stared directly at Luna.

"Come out of the cold, my pretty one, and sit by the fire," Mystia purred.

Luna approached cautiously and sat down across from the witch.

"To what do I owe the honor of this royal visit?" the witch asked. The flickering firelight made the crags and scars of her stony face look like deep canyons.

"I think you already know," said Luna sharply.

The witch didn't bat an eyelash at the princess's impudence. "Indeed, I do," she said, stirring her thickening broth slowly. "These rheumy eyes of mine still have the Sight. I've watched you and your sister grow, Princess Luna. Her beauty is well known throughout the land, much like *your* temper and impertinence."

"I don't have time for a lecture from you, old woman. I am in need of a magic spell. Give it to me, or I shall have your miserable cottage burned to the ground!"

"Aye, you could do that." The witch's gaze blackened. "But I wouldn't if I were you." After a few moments of letting her warning sink in, Mystia's face softened and she asked lightly, "What is it your heart desires, my Lady?"

Luna looked the witch in the eye. "My parents do not notice me! They love Olivia more than life itself. I am invisible to them; a ghost; perhaps, even, a regret! I want them to see *me* for who I am and love me as they do my sister!" She swiped at a tear that slipped down her cheek.

The old witch smiled.

"As you wish, my dear," the witch said. "I have observed how you've lived your life in your sister's shadow, and what a burden it must be! With only a palace to spend your days in, and servants to wait on your every need. You are clearly a damsel in distress. I shall mix a potion for you at once. Wait here."

The witch shuffled away into her cottage, leaving Luna to wait out in the cold. When the old hag returned, she was holding a small cup. Wisps of steam rose from the liquid within. The scent made Luna's nose wrinkle as she took it from the witch.

"It smells disgusting," she complained, as she brought it to her lips.

"Drink every drop, and then return to your bed chamber to sleep. When you awake in the morning, no one will look at you the same again."

Luna did as the old crone instructed, gagging on the dregs at the bottom. The flavor and consistency reminded her of seaweed she once ate on a dare when she was seven, only with the bitter aftertaste of coriander and wormwood. When she was finished, she dropped the cup to the ground, turned away from Luna without a word, and staggered back to the castle. Upon reaching her chamber, she threw herself into bed and tried to ignore her complaining stomach. Exhausted, she fell into a deep sleep.

When she awoke, the sun was a blot of red melted wax in the east. Eager to view the beauty that must be radiating from every pore in her skin, Luna dashed to the nearest mirror. To her horror, she found the image that stared back at her to be more hideous than Luna herself. She screamed at the oozing sores and ugly black pock marks scattered across her face.

When her family heard her pitiful wailing, they burst into her chamber and cried out in alarm. "Oh, Luna," sobbed her mother, throwing her arms around her daughter. "What has happened to you? Who has done this to you?"

Luna choked back her tears and said, "It was Mystia, the old crone of the woods. I went to visit her last night, and she cursed me! I was merely paying her a visit—now look what she's done!"

"What I did was exactly what Princess Luna demanded of me," came a scolding voice behind them. Mystia lurched into the room and pointed her heavy oaken walking stick at Luna. "You wanted attention? Now I've given it to you. See what jealousy gets you, my pretty."

"Release her from your curse, miserable old hag, or I shall have your head!" roared the King.

"Impossible, sire. Magic of this sort only travels one way, you see. But I make you a proposal. I shall put your daughter out of her misery, and at the same time teach a lesson to the people of Nightville. No longer shall their nights be so dark and brooding. They shall have light to see by as they walk the straight and narrow path of life. But should they find themselves tempted to consort with dark magic, they need only to look up at the blemished face of your daughter riding her midnight chariot to remind them of the consequences."

"Do it," begged Luna, "I cannot live this way."

With the King and Queen's blessings, Mystia put Luna to sleep forever. Her face became the moon which emblazoned the night sky. All who gazed upon it said a silent blessing and made sure to teach their children to avoid wickedness and embrace love.

The children listened, and Mystia was never seen or heard from again.

$$\sim\!\!\sim$$

INDEPENDENT WORK—Theme and Main Idea

Directions: Identify the theme and main idea in "The Witch of Nightville" on your own. Then answer a couple more questions.

SUBJECT: _____

THEME: _____

MAIN IDEA: _____

_____

1. Was this story fantasy or realistic? _____ How do you know? _____

_____

2. Make a prediction: What will life be like in Nightville after what happened to Luna? _____

_____

Summarizing

A summary captures the most important details of the book, chapter or paragraph in your own words. A summary is NOT a retell of all the major events of a story. This is trickier.

A good summary shares a little from the beginning, a little from the middle, and a little from the end. Just enough to understand the story's plot. It includes key details about the character, too. **It should be no longer than about 2-3 sentences maximum.**

It does NOT include minor supporting details—such as the color of the main character's hair or what she ate for breakfast that morning—nor does it tell us what the theme or main idea might be.

We're going to learn the **SWBST** summarizing strategy, introduced by James Macon, Diane Bewell, and MaryEllen Vogt in their 1991 booklet *Responses to Literature*. We use this for narratives with problem/solution plot structures.

Somebody
Wants
But
So
Then

Vocabulary Review
synonym
fiction
narrative
realistic
fantasy
text structure
plot
setting
cause/effect
sequence
visualize
inference
trait
figurative language
theme
main idea
summarize

How does this strategy work? Glad you asked! Let's summarize "Barney the Barn Cat" using SWBST.

Somebody	Barney the Barn Cat
Wants	to get rid of the dog in his barn
But	he is afraid of the dog
So	the mice agree to help him
Then	Barney and the mice live happily ever after.

Let's put it all together and see how it sounds!

Barney the Barn Cat wants to get rid of a dog in his barn, but he is afraid of the dog. So, the mice agree to help him. Then Barney and the mice live happily ever after.

That was fun, wasn't it? Re-read "The Witch of Nightville" and summarize Luna's story using SWBST.

Somebody	
Wants	
But	
So	
Then	

Write your summary statement in the box below!

The Witch of Nightville

Princess Luna lived with her family in a sparkling castle high above the tiny hamlet of Nightville. Luna was the younger of two sisters, and at fourteen, also the most disobedient. She was a petty girl, who spent long hours staring at her plain face in the palace mirror, and daydreaming about love, glory, and riches. She was also bitterly jealous of her older sister, the lovely and graceful Princess Olivia, who was due to be wed in a fortnight.

One evening Luna stood outside her sister's bedchamber. She listened as her mother told Olivia about the upcoming wedding.

"It will be so *lovely*," boasted the Queen. "Thousands of roses, dahlias, and hydrangeas will transform our courtyard into the garden of Eden. The finest minstrels and musicians from all over the land will entertain us. All the kings and queens from the Seven Kingdoms will be in attendance, and your stunning beauty will mesmerize them."

When Luna heard this, her rage boiled.

She stormed away and returned to her own bedchamber. She spent the rest of the evening plotting her revenge.

Since the early days, Luna's mother and father clearly favored Olivia. Olivia had the sort of beauty that stopped conversation when she walked into a room. Her eyes sparkled like sapphires and her smile made strangers forget what they were going to say. By contrast, Luna was a forgettable sort of pretty. With her smatter of freckles, brown eyes, and intensely shy personality, she was easy to overlook. No matter how many Latin texts she learned to read or stallions she learned to ride, Luna failed to impress her royal parents. Their lives revolved around Olivia. Nothing would ever change that fact.

About an hour later she heard a knock at her door. "May I come in?" asked Olivia.

"What do you want?" grumbled Luna.

"I came to see if you were all right," she said. "Ever since I announced my marriage plans to Prince Randolph, you've been so distant around me. I want you to be happy, that is all."

Luna rolled over in her bed and glared at her. "You really want to make me happy?"

Her sister nodded. "More than anything!"

"Then you'll get out and leave me alone forever. You think you're so special, marrying a prince and all, but you'll see. Someday, very soon, I'll be the one everyone is talking about. My beauty will light up this world and no one will forget who I am!"

"One day, Luna, you will find the prince of your dreams, too."

Luna scoffed. "He will probably be a toad of a man and his castle half the size of Randolph's."

Princess Olivia looked stricken. "I'm sorry you feel that way," she said quietly, closing the door. *Yes, you will be sorry*, thought Luna.

After night dropped its cloak over the world and the sky bloomed with stars, Luna approached the Outer Gate. She ordered the startled guards—who rarely heard the demure princess speak—to lower the gate and fetch her horse. She was sure the answer to all her problems would be found in the Forest of Magic. And she would do whatever it took to convince the witch who lived there to help her.

Princess Luna spurred her horse and it took off like a shot into the forest. After several minutes of hard riding through the near pitch-black woods, she paused to let the horse rest. All around her she heard the flutter of bats and the whine of insects in her ears. With no light from above but the cold glimmer of stars, Luna could barely see her hands in front of her face.

Suddenly, her heartbeat spiked when she heard what sounded like singing coming from up ahead. Only it wasn't a tune that a traveling minstrel might sing; it was the screechy voice of the old crone Mystia, who resided in the heart of the forest.

As Luna came closer to the singing, she stopped and dismounted. Through the thickets, Luna spied the witch hunched over a cooking fire, a wooden spoon held inches from her mouth, about to taste the broth. But the old woman didn't move; she stared directly at Luna.

"Come out of the cold, my pretty one, and sit by the fire," Mystia purred.

Luna approached cautiously and sat down across from the witch.

"To what do I owe the honor of this royal visit?" the witch asked. The flickering firelight made the crags and scars of her stony face look like deep canyons.

"I think you already know," said Luna sharply.

The witch didn't bat an eyelash at the princess's impudence. "Indeed, I do," she said, stirring her thickening broth slowly. "These rheumy eyes of mine still have the Sight. I've watched you and your sister grow, Princess Luna. Her beauty is well known throughout the land, much like *your* temper and impertinence."

"I don't have time for a lecture from you, old woman. I am in need of a magic spell. Give it to me, or I shall have your miserable cottage burned to the ground!"

"Aye, you could do that." The witch's gaze blackened. "But I wouldn't if I were you." After a few moments of letting her warning sink in, Mystia's face softened and she asked lightly, "What is it your heart desires, my Lady?"

Luna looked the witch in the eye. "My parents do not notice me! They love Olivia more than life itself. I am invisible to them; a ghost; perhaps, even, a regret! I want them to see *me* for who I am and love me as they do my sister!" She swiped at a tear that slipped down her cheek.

The old witch smiled.

"As you wish, my dear," the witch said. "I have observed how you've lived your life in your sister's shadow, and what a burden it must be! With only a palace to spend your days in, and servants to wait on your every need. You are clearly a damsel in distress. I shall mix a potion for you at once. Wait here."

The witch shuffled away into her cottage, leaving Luna to wait out in the cold. When the old hag returned, she was holding a small cup. Wisps of steam rose from the liquid within. The scent made Luna's nose wrinkle as she took it from the witch.

"It smells disgusting," she complained, as she brought it to her lips.

"Drink every drop, and then return to your bed chamber to sleep. When you awake in the morning, no one will look at you the same again."

Luna did as the old crone instructed, gagging on the dregs at the bottom. The flavor and consistency reminded her of seaweed she once ate on a dare when she was seven, only with the bitter aftertaste of coriander and wormwood. When she was finished, she dropped the cup to the ground, turned away from Luna without a word, and staggered back to the castle. Upon reaching her chamber, she threw herself into bed and tried to ignore her complaining stomach. Exhausted, she fell into a deep sleep.

When she awoke, the sun was a blot of red melted wax in the east. Eager to view the beauty that must be radiating from every pore in her skin, Luna dashed to the nearest mirror. To her horror, she found the image that stared back at her to be more hideous than Luna herself. She screamed at the oozing sores and ugly black pock marks scattered across her face.

When her family heard her pitiful wailing, they burst into her chamber and cried out in alarm. "Oh, Luna," sobbed her mother, throwing her arms around her daughter. "What has happened to you? Who has done this to you?"

Luna choked back her tears and said, "It was Mystia, the old crone of the woods. I went to visit her last night, and she cursed me! I was merely paying her a visit—now look what she's done!"

"What I did was exactly what Princess Luna demanded of me," came a scolding voice behind them. Mystia lurched into the room and pointed her heavy oaken walking stick at Luna. "You wanted attention? Now I've given it to you. See what jealousy gets you, my pretty."

"Release her from your curse, miserable old hag, or I shall have your head!" roared the King.

"Impossible, sire. Magic of this sort only travels one way, you see. But I make you a proposal. I shall put your daughter out of her misery, and at the same time teach a lesson to the people of Nightville. No longer shall their nights be so dark and brooding. They shall have light to see by as they walk the straight and narrow path of life. But should they find themselves tempted to consort with dark magic, they need only to look up at the blemished face of your daughter riding her midnight chariot to remind them of the consequences."

"Do it," begged Luna, "I cannot live this way."

With the King and Queen's blessings, Mystia put Luna to sleep forever. Her face became the moon which emblazoned the night sky. All who gazed upon it said a silent blessing and made sure to teach their children to avoid wickedness and embrace love.

The children listened, and Mystia was never seen or heard from again.

Website Woes

Gina Murphy was exhausted when she got home from school. Her sixth-grade computer teacher had assigned the class a long project to do over the weekend—design a website! How was she going to finish it by Monday? She was so worried, her stomach started to cramp. When she got home, she plopped in a chair in the living room and closed her eyes.

"Everything all right?" she heard her mother ask.

Gina opened her eyes. Her head pounded with a headache.

"Not really," she admitted. Her mom sat down across from her, and Gina told her all about the assignment.

"Oh, that's okay," Mrs. Murphy said. "I can help you."

"This project is going to take me forever!" Gina groaned, turning away. "I barely know how to type on a computer!"

"Why don't you rest a while," suggested Mrs. Murphy, "and we'll talk about it more over dinner. I have a few ideas."

Gina's mouth watered when she smelled something spicy wafting from the kitchen. "What are we having?"

"Your favorite—spaghetti and meatballs!"

At dinner, Gina's parents helped her plan for her computer project.

"You know, your father and I both work for a tech firm, so we know a lot about websites and how they work."

Gina's eyes grew wide. "You do? I thought you just typed stuff all day."

Mr. Murphy laughed as he pushed his empty plate aside. "We do that, too. But I also write software programs that run many of our company's systems. Your mother works on our company's cyber security programs to be sure all of our data is secure. Big league stuff, kiddo."

Wow. Gina had never really asked what her parents did all day, except she knew they drove to work at a big shiny building in the middle of the city. And worked on computers.

"So, you guys can help me design a website?"

"You betcha," said Mrs. Murphy. "We'll get to it right away!"

After dishes were washed and put away, Mr. and Mrs. Murphy led Gina to her mother's office. They let her sit at her mother's enormous desk and turn on the computer.

"You design a website using a platform," explained Mrs. Murphy as she logged in. "An example of an easy platform to use is Weebly."

"That's right," added Mr. Murphy. "You can build a website for free using Weebly and add lots of cool features to it. Check it out."

Together, Gina's mother and father showed her all the background designs and layout options for her website. Gina chose colors and themes, and then she typed a short description about herself for the home page. Later, her mother promised to show her how to upload photographs and text.

"Thank you so much for your help, guys," Gina said with a smile.

"Anytime," said her mother. "There's just one more thing. Your website needs a domain name, an address to type into the search engine to find it. What do you want to call your website?"

Gina thought for a moment. "I think I have a great idea!" She started typing www.ginahastwogreatparents.com.

Laughing, her parents high-fived her and agreed it was a great name.

Somebody	
Wants	
But	
So	
Then	

Write your summary statement of "Website Woes" below!

Vocabulary Review

Congratulations! You made it to the end of Part One—and you're still in one piece! We just have one more piece of business before we conclude this section of the book. Choose words from the box below to fill in the blanks.

See you in Part 2!

synonym	fiction	narrative	realistic	fantasy	text structure
plot	setting	cause/effect	sequence	visualize	inference
trait	summarize	text-based answer		figurative language	

1. A _____ is a real or made-up story.

2. The _____ of a narrative is what happens in the beginning, middle, and end.

3. If you're looking for a new word that means the same or almost the same as the old word, then you're looking for a _____.

4. When something happens because of something else, that is an example of _____.

5. When something isn't obvious, you may need to use your background knowledge plus the text itself to make an _____ about what's going on.

6. A _____ needs a quote from the text.

7. When you're listing the major events of a story from beginning to end, you are writing a _____.

8. The _____ of most stories is problem/solution.

9. Where and when a narrative takes place is called _____.

10. A type of narrative where all the events are made up is _____.

11. When you _____, don't tell everything that happened in the story, just state the most important information.

12. A character's _____ is a quality that we see by the character's actions and words.

13. Authors write descriptively so we can _____ the plot of the story.

14. A _____ story is one where the characters and plot could happen in real life.

15. When a story features characters or events that are not found in real life, we call it _____.

16. An example of _____ would be "Her hair was like golden strands of silk."

PART 2

Organizational Aids and Graphic Organizers for Reading and Writing, Answer Key, Note-taking Pages

In each box below, copy a passage from the book or article you're reading that has a word whose meaning you're unsure of.

A synonym for _____ might be_____

What were your clue words? _____

A synonym for _____ might be_____

What were your clue words? _____

In each box below, copy a passage from the book or article you're reading that has tricky words to pronounce. Then write the words on the lines below and decode them with your new reading strategy.

_____   _____

_____   _____

_____   _____

_____   _____

INDEPENDENT WORK—Character, Plot and Setting

In the box below, copy a passage from the story you're reading that describes the setting. Be sure to include a character, too.

In the box below, write two examples of plot events happening in your story. This means two different actions that the characters are taking.

1

2

Fill in three cause and effect examples from the story you're reading.

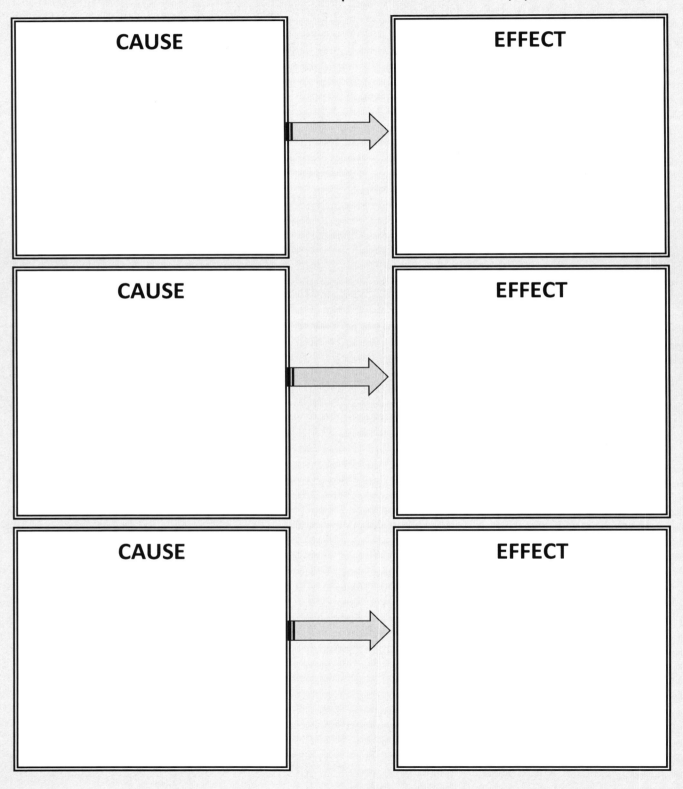

BEGINNING

(include the setting)

In the beginning,

MIDDLE

Next,

Then,

After,

END

In the end,

In the box below, write an excerpt from your story that shows your main character's traits.

A character trait of _____ is _____.

What background knowledge and text clues helped you know this?

Background Knowledge	Text Evidence

Somebody	
Wants	
But	
So	
Then	

Write the summary statement of the text you're reading below!

Directions: In the two boxes below, write sentences containing figurative language from the book you're reading.

Type of figurative language (circle one)

hyperbole   simile   metaphor   idiom   personification

Type of figurative language (circle one)

hyperbole   simile   metaphor   idiom   personification

Story Map

Directions: Use this graphic organizer to review the basic elements of a story you've read or plan your own story!

Title _____

Author _____

Characters

Setting

Problem

3 Main Events

-
-
-

Resolution

Story Map Interview

Directions: Use this graphic organizer to think through your plot a little deeper.

What is the story about?

What are some qualities of your main character?

What problem did he/she face?

How did he/she react to the problem?

How was the problem resolved?

Circle Plot Graphic Organizer

Name:

Title:

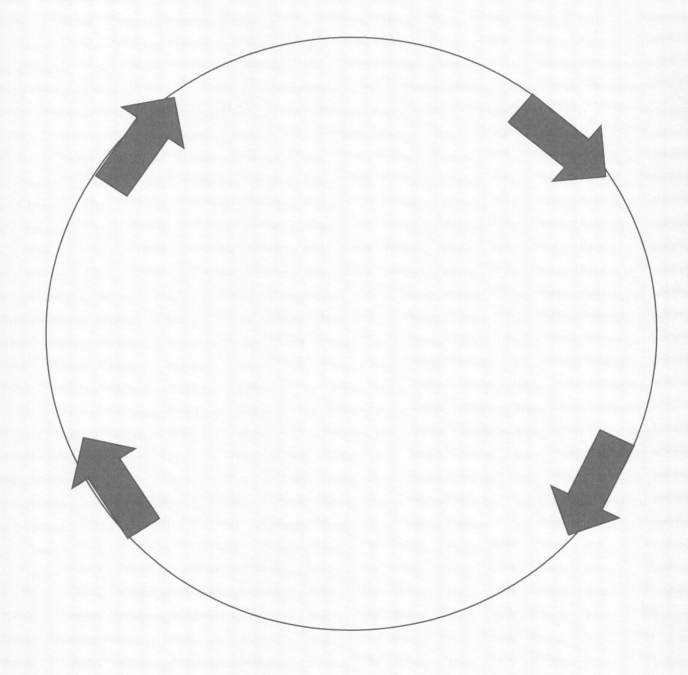

Framing-Question Story Map

Directions: Use this graphic organizer to review the basic elements of a framing-question story you've read or plan your own story!

Title _____

Author _____

Characters	Setting	Problem

Framing Question

3 Main Events

-
-
-

Resolution

Personal Narrative Map

Directions: Use this graphic organizer to list the key details of an experience a character has had or to plan a personal narrative.

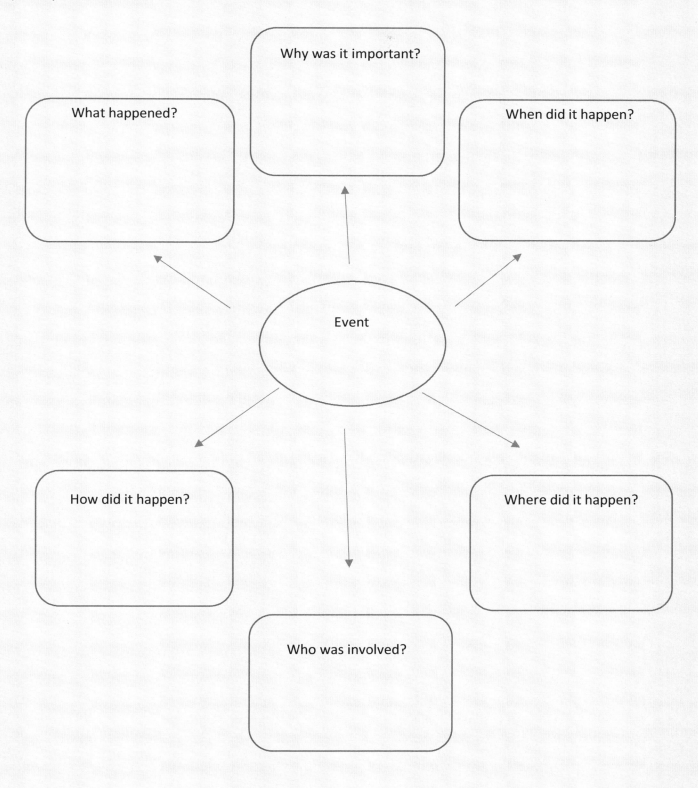

Diary Entry Map

Directions: Use this map to write the dates and major events in a diary-structured story or for planning your own story!

Date:

Characters:

Date:

Date:

Date:

Resolution:

Answer Key

Page 3

1) rude; clue words: impolite, no respect, poor manners
2) dangerous; clue words: dangerous, deadly
3) land; clue words: mountains, quick sand

Page 10

overcome	conversation	dictionary
macaroni	refreshment	raspberry
strawberry	gingerbread	reflection
refrigerate	mountain	uncommon
resistance	indecisively	adversely
watermelon	helicopter	musical
alphabetize	revolution	immunity

Page 20

1. Gina
2. The teacher assigned Gina to create a website.

3. Gina is so exhausted because it was Friday and she was worried about her school project.
4. Answers may vary:

    Gina's parents helped her design a website. Gina's mother told her, "Your father and I both work for a tech firm, so we know a lot about websites and how they work." They showed Gina different platforms to use like Wix and how to design the website. In the end, Gina was so thankful for her parents' help that she named the website after them!

Page 25

1. Realistic story: A Trunk of Trouble
2. Fantasy story: The Fox and the Crow
3. (Answers may vary) You can tell the difference between the two stories because animals talk in The Fox and the Crow.

Page 33

1. The setting changed when Carrie's family drove their house to Fury Mountain theme park.
2. Realistic; I know it's realistic because families like Carrie's go to theme parks all the time.
3. The beginning event was Carrie jumping out of bed before the alarm clock woke her because she was so excited.
4. The plot complication was Carrie suddenly became nervous when she saw the huge roller coaster and almost didn't ride it.
5. The solution to the problem was Carrie's dad took her on the roller coaster instead of her brother.
6. The story ended with Carrie proud of herself that she rode the roller coaster and eager to do it again.
7. The text structure is problem and solution.

Page 37
Cause: She was nervous
Effect: She ignored him
Cause: Olivia played very well

Page 39 Possible answers:
Cause: Ant stored away food.
Effect: He had plenty for winter.

Cause: Grasshopper played.
Effect: He didn't have food for winter.

Cause: Grasshopper didn't have food for winter.
Effect: He learned he should prepare for days of necessity.

Page 44
Next, Alex let's out a little cry.
After, Alex has a scary dream about his house flooding with water.

Page 46
In the beginning, a group of people help Professor Feathers search for the missing children.
Next, the owl spots a crevasse in the ice.
Then, the owl flies down into the hole in the ice.
After, he hurts his wing on the ice.
In the end, he finds Alex and Olivia stuck in the ice.

Page 47
1. The main character of this story is Professor Feathers.
2. Fantasy. I know it's fantasy because owls don't rescue children stuck in ice.
3. Problem and solution
4. Answers may vary:

Cause: Owl flies into crack in the ice.
Effect: He hurts his wing

Page 49
1. The zoo
2. Answers vary. Background knowledge: you have to go to a zoo to see the animals listed in the text. Text evidence: "She wouldn't want to miss the opportunity to take pictures of the tigers, crocodiles, or polar bears."
3. Excited; enthusiastic; worried
4. Answers vary. Background knowledge: She must care a lot for this trip since she keeps checking her backpack. Text evidence: "Sara checked her backpack for the third time to make sure she had everything she needed for the field trip: a notebook, two pencils, her permission slip, and a camera.

Page 50
1. They love him
2. Answers vary. Background knowledge: They keep lots of pictures of him, so they must really love him. Text evidence: "… and now the photographs showed a large blond boy riding his first bicycle, on a carousel at the fair, playing a computer game with his father, being hugged and kissed by his mother."

Page 51
1. They do not love Harry.
2. Answers vary. Background knowledge: It's rude to wake somebody up the way Aunt Petunia did. Text evidence: "His Aunt Petunia was awake and it was her shrill voice that made the first noise of the day."

Page 61
1. Realistic
2. Problem and solution
3. The setting of the story was a park in Brooklyn, New York.
4. In the beginning, Annabelle gets dressed up for Halloween. Next, her mom takes her trick or treating in the neighborhood. Then, they find kids playing in a park and discover an old stone house. After, they explore inside the old house. In the end, Annabelle sees a ghost and decides to keep it a secret.
5. A character trait that describes Annabelle is curiosity because she's new to the city and wants to explore.

Page 64
1. idiom
2. simile
3. personification
4. metaphor
5. hyperbole
6. idiom
7. metaphor

Page 69
1. Her own stomach, in fact, growled at her daily like a caged animal.
2. Acceptable answers: simile or hyperbole
3. "They're eating us out of house and home!"

Pages 76-77   Answers vary
1. Cooperation
2. Working together can achieve your goals
3. Barney the barn cat and the mice make a plan to scare a mean dog away from the barn.

4. Fantasy. I know this story is fantasy because mice and cats don't talk or work together to set traps.
5. Problem and solution
6. Both Barney and the mice will get to relax because the dog won't be back anymore.
7. Cause: A dog sniffs around the barn. Effect: Barney and the mice come up with a plan to get rid of the dog for good.

Page 83 Answers vary
1. Jealousy
2. Being jealous of others can lead to our own downfall.
3. Princess Luna wants to be beautiful like her sister and makes a deal with a witch that makes her ugly instead.
4. Fantasy. It is fantasy because there are no such thing as witches and the moon is not actually someone's face.
5. In Nightville, they will have light to see by at night and everyone will remember the terrible thing that Luna did.

Page 86
Luna
Wants all the attention that her sister gets
But she isn't as beautiful as her sister, Olivia
So Luna visits the witch Mystia for a magic potion
Then the potion backfires and makes Luna very ugly.

Luna wants the attention that her sister gets, but she isn't as beautiful as Olivia. So, Luna visits the witch Mystia for a magic potion. Then the potion backfires and makes Luna very ugly.

Page 94
Gina
Wants help with her homework project

But she doesn't know how to make a website
So her parents show her how to do it
Then Gina names the website after them

Gina wants help with her homework project, but she doesn't know how to make a website. So, her parents show her how to do it. Then Gina names the website after them.

Page 95-96
1. Narrative
2. plot
3. synonym
4. cause/effect
5. inference
6. text-based answer
7. sequence
8. text structure
9. setting
10. fiction
11. summarize
12. trait
13. visualize
14. realistic
15. fantasy
16. figurative language

NOTES

NOTES

ABOUT THE AUTHOR

David R. Smith lives in Livonia, NY with his wife and two children. He is a teacher in the Canandaigua City School District. Ever since he was a young boy he's been reading and writing fiction. He loves a good fantasy or ghost story. His favorite authors include Ray Bradbury, Neil Gaiman, Mary Downing Hahn, and Stephen King. He's won numerous fiction writing contests. His stories have appeared in e-zines and magazines.